T0081768

Easy Concert Pieces
Leichte Konzertstücke

for Guitar
für Gitarre

Volume 1 / Band 1

Edited by / Herausgegeben von
Peter Ansorge, Bruno Szordikowski
and / und Martin Hegel

ED 21636D
ISMN 979-0-001-21678-4

Volume 2 / Band 2
ED 21637D

Volume 3 / Band 3
ED 22558

Cover illustration:
Light cone: © PROBilder – Fotolia.com

www.schott-music.com

Mainz · London · Madrid · Paris · New York · Tokyo · Beijing
© 2013/2022 Schott Music GmbH & Co. KG, Mainz · Printed in Germany

Contents and Track List / Inhalt und Tracklist

Tuning notes / Stimmtöne (a = 440 Hz)

55 e
56 b (h)
57 g
58 d
59 A
60 E

Recording/Einspielung:
Fabian Hinsche, Martin Hegel (Guitar)
℗ 2013 Schott Music & Media GmbH, Mainz, Germany

Please visit **www.schott-music.com/online-material** to download all audio files for free using the following voucher code: **USPyM5EV**

Auf der Website **www.schott-music.com/online-material** können alle Audio-Dateien mit dem folgenden Gutscheincode kostenlos heruntergeladen werden: **USPyM5EV**

Track 1

That sound is so lovely
Das klinget so herrlich

Wolfgang Amadeus Mozart
(1756–1791)
Arr.: Martin Hegel

*) Original: a'

from / aus: The Magic Flute / Die Zauberflöte, KV 620

Track 2

Il Canario

Cesare Negri
(1535–1604)

from / aus: Le Gratie d'Amore

© 2013 Schott Music GmbH & Co. KG, Mainz

Andante

Track 3

Joseph Küffner
(1776–1856)
Arr.: Peter Ansorge,
Bruno Szordikowski

Dance

Tanz

Track 4

Henry Purcell
(1659–1695)
Arr.: Peter Ansorge,
Bruno Szordikowski

from / aus: The Fairy Queen

Track 5

Hungarian Dance
Ungarischer Tanz

Anonymus
Arr.: Peter Ansorge,
Bruno Szordikowski

Little Dutch Dance
Ein niderlendisch Tentzlein

Hans Neusiedler
(1508–1563)

Track 6

from / aus: H. Neusiedler, The First Book / Das erste Buch 1544

Track 7

The Trout
Die Forelle

Franz Schubert
(1797–1828)
Arr.: Martin Hegel

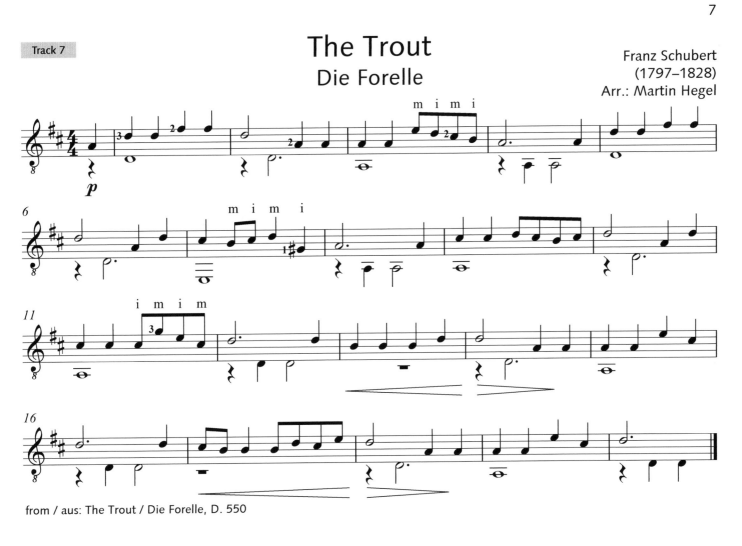

from / aus: The Trout / Die Forelle, D. 550

Track 8

Vienna Blood
Wiener Blut

Johann Strauss (Sohn)
(1825–1899)
Arr.: Martin Hegel

from / aus: Waltz for Orchestra / Konzertwalzer, op. 354

Track 9

Radetzky March
Radetzky-Marsch

Johann Strauss (Vater)
(1804–1849)
Arr.: Martin Hegel

from / aus: Radetzky March / Radetzky-Marsch, op. 228

Track 10

Ode to Joy
Freude schöner Götterfunken

Ludwig van Beethoven
(1770–1827)
Arr.: Martin Hegel

from / aus: Symphony No. 9 / Sinfonie Nr. 9, op. 125

The Old Castle
Das alte Schloss

Modest Mussorgsky
(1839–1881)
Arr.: Martin Hegel

from / aus: Pictures at an Exhibition / Bilder einer Ausstellung

La Réjouissance

Track 12

Georg Friedrich Händel
(1685–1759)
Arr.: Martin Hegel

from / aus: Music for the Royal Fireworks / Feuerwerksmusik, HWV 351

Autumn

Der Herbst

Track 13

Antonio Vivaldi
(1678–1741)
Arr.: Martin Hegel

from / aus: The Four Seasons / Die vier Jahreszeiten

Minuet
Menuet

Track 14

Robert de Visée
(1660–1720)
Arr.: Peter Ansorge,
Bruno Szordikowski

Romance
Romanze

Track 15

Wolfgang Amadeus Mozart
(1756–1791)
Arr.: Martin Hegel

from / aus: Little Night Music / Eine kleine Nachtmusik, KV 525

Track 16

Lullaby
Wiegenlied

Johannes Brahms
(1833–1897)
Arr.: Martin Hegel

from / aus: Five Songs / Fünf Lieder, op. 49

Track 17

Andante

Joseph Haydn
(1732–1809)
Arr.: Martin Hegel

from / aus: Symphony No. 94 "Surprise" / Sinfonie Nr. 94 „Mit dem Paukenschlag"

Track 18

Spanish Romance
Spanische Romanze

Anonymus
Arr.: Peter Ansorge,
Bruno Szordikowski

Fine

D. C. al Fine

Track 19

Moderato

Anton Diabelli
(1781–1858)

from / aus: Very Easy Exercises / 30 sehr leichte Übungsstücke, op. 39

14

for Kevin
Rondo

Track 20

Bruno Szordikowski
(*1944)

for Ik Bum

Study / Studie

Bruno Szordikowski
(*1944)

Track 21

D. C. al Fine

Track 22

In the Fifth Position

Flowing

Reginald Smith Brindle
(1917–2003)

from / aus: Guitarcosmos 1 (1979), Schott ED 11387

Track 23

Andantino

Dionisio Aguado
(1784–1849)
Arr.: Peter Ansorge,
Bruno Szordikowski

Track 24

German Dance
Deutscher Tanz
(„Was sollen wir auf den Abend tun?")

Anonymus
(Fabricius' Lute Book)
Arr.: Peter Ansorge,
Bruno Szordikowski

Track 25

Italian Dance
Italienischer Tanz

(Schiarazula Marazula)

Giorgio Mainerio
(ca. 1540–1582)
Arr.: Peter Ansorge,
Bruno Szordikowski

Track 26

Two Country Dances
Zwei Kontratänze

John Playford
(1623–1686)
Arr.: Peter Ansorge,
Bruno Szordikowski

I

Track 27

II

from / aus: The English Dancing Master

Fine

D. C. al Fine

Greensleeves

Anonymus
(16th century)
Arr.: Martin Hegel

Paradetas

Track 29

Gaspar Sanz
(1640–1710)

Aeolian Mode

Track 30

Reginald Smith Brindle
(1917–2003)

Andante con moto

Fine

D. C. al Fine

from/aus: Guitarcosmos 1 (1979), Schott ED 11387

Spagnoletta

Track 31

Anonymus
Arr.: Peter Ansorge,
Bruno Szordikowski

Cancan

Jacques Offenbach
(1819–1880)
Arr.: Martin Hegel

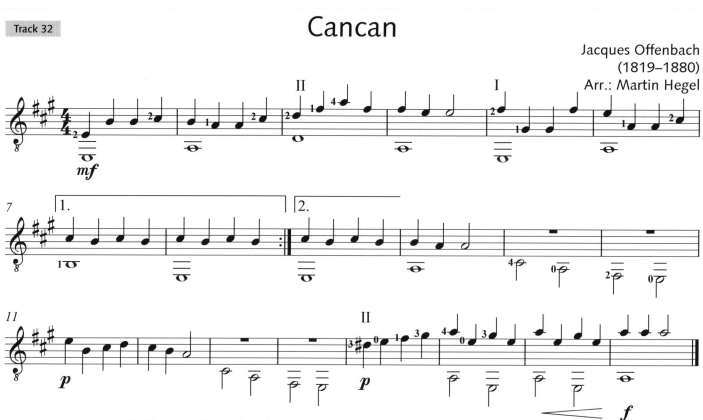

from / aus: Orpheus in the Underworld / Orpheus in der Unterwelt

Baltic Dance
Baltischer Tanz

from a Baltic Lute Book
Arr.: Peter Ansorge,
Bruno Szordikowski

Siciliana

from / aus: op. 59

Matteo Carcassi
(1792–1853)

William Tell

Wilhelm Tell

Gioachino Rossini
(1792–1868)
Arr.: Martin Hegel

from / aus: William Tell / Wilhelm Tell

The Barber of Seville
Der Barbier von Sevilla

Track 36

Gioachino Rossini
(1792–1868)
Arr.: Martin Hegel

from / aus: The Barber of Seville / Der Barbier von Sevilla

Cancion

Track 37

Gaspar Sanz
(1640–1710)

from / aus: Libro segundo, de cifras sobre la guitarra española

Track 38

French Dance
Französischer Tanz
(Tourdion)

after Pierre Attaignant
(ca. 1494–1551/52)
Arr.: Peter Ansorge,
Bruno Szordikowski

Track 39

Prélude
(Eurovision Melody / Eurovisions-Melodie)

Marc-Antoine Charpentier
(ca. 1643–1704)
Arr.: Peter Ansorge,
Bruno Szordikowski

from / aus: Te Deum

Minuet
Menuett

Johann Philipp Krieger
(1649–1725)
Arr.: Peter Ansorge,
Bruno Szordikowski

Track 40

Minuet
Menuett

Johann Anton Logy
(ca. 1650–1721)
Arr.: Peter Ansorge,
Bruno Szordikowski

Track 41

Adagio

Johann Sebastian Bach
(1685–1750)
Arr.: Martin Hegel

Track 42

from / aus: J. S. Bach, Concerto for Harpsichord (after Marcello) / Cembalo-Konzert (nach Marcello), BWV 974

Minuet
Menuett

Silvius Leopold Weiss
(1686–1750)

Track 43

from / aus: Suite D minor / d-Moll

Track 44

Ah, vous dirai-je, Maman
(Theme / Thema)

Wolfgang Amadeus Mozart
(1756–1791)
Arr.: Martin Hegel

Fine

D. C. al Fine

from / aus: Variations on / Variationen über "Ah, vous dirai-je, Maman", KV 265

Track 45

Winter

Antonio Vivaldi
(1678–1741)
Arr.: Martin Hegel

from / aus: The Four Seasons / Die vier Jahreszeiten

Track 46

Birdcatcher's Aria
Arie des Vogelfängers

Wolfgang Amadeus Mozart
(1756–1791)
Arr.: Martin Hegel

from / aus: The Magic Flute / Die Zauberflöte, KV 620

Track 47

Hungarian Dance No. 5
Ungarischer Tanz Nr. 5

Johannes Brahms
(1833–1897)
Arr.: Martin Hegel

from / aus: 21 Hungarian dances / 21 Ungarische Tänze

Track 48

Mr. Dowland's Midnight

John Dowland
(1562–1626)

Bourrée

Ernst Gottlieb Baron
(1696–1760)
Arr.: Peter Ansorge,
Bruno Szordikowski

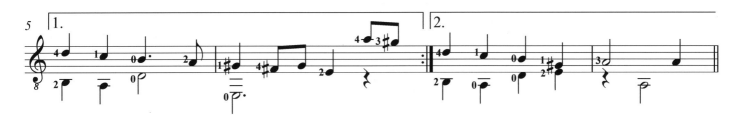

*) Original:

Track 50

Song of the Toreadors
Lied der Toreadore

Georges Bizet
(1838–1875)
Arr.: Martin Hegel

from / aus: Carmen

Track 51

Chorus of the Hebrew Slaves
Gefangenenchor

Giuseppe Verdi
(1813–1901)
Arr.: Martin Hegel

from / aus: Nabucco

Musette

Track 52

Johann Sebastian Bach
(1685–1750)
Arr.: Martin Hegel

from / aus: Notebook for / Notenbüchlein für Anna Magdalena Bach

D. C. al Fine

Moderato cantabile

Track 53

Frédéric Chopin
(1810–1849)
Arr.: Martin Hegel

from / aus: Fantasie Impromptu, op. 66

Track 54

March of the Toreadors

Marsch der Toreadore

George Bizet
(1838–1875)
Arr.: Martin Hegel

from / aus: Carmen

Schott Music, Mainz 55 611